W9-AEH-246

WORD PROBLEMS
USING
MULTIPLICATION
AND
DIVISION

MASTERING MATH WORD PROBLEMS

Zella Williams and
Rebecca Wingard-Nelson

Enslow Publishing
101 W. 23rd Street
Suite 240
New York, NY 10011
USA

enslow.com

Published in 2017 by Enslow Publishing, LLC.
101 W. 23rd Street, Suite 240, New York, NY 10011

Library of Congress Cataloging-in-Publication Data

Names: Williams, Zella, author. | Wingard-Nelson, Rebecca, author.
Title: Word Problems Using Multiplication and Division / Zella Williams and Rebecca Wingard-Nelson.
Description: New York : Enslow Publishing, 2017 | Series: Mastering math word problems | Includes bibliographical references and index.
Identifiers: ISBN 9780766082649 (pbk.) | ISBN 9780766082663 (library bound) | ISBN 9780766082656 (6 pack) | ISBN 978-0-7660-8264-9 (pbk.)
Subjects: LCSH: Multiplication—Juvenile literature. | Division—Juvenile literature. | Word problems (Mathematics)—Juvenile literature. | Problem solving—Juvenile literature.
Classification: LCC QA115.W564 2017 | DDC 513.2'13—dc23

Printed in China

To Our Readers: We have done our best to make sure all websites in this book were active and appropriate when we went to press. However, the author and the publisher have no control over and assume no liability for the material available on those websites or on any websites they may link to. Any comments or suggestions can be sent by email to customerservice@enslow.com.

Portions of this book originally appeared in the book *Big Truck and Car Word Problems Starring Multiplication and Division*.

Photo Credits: Cover, p. 1 Terry Vine/Blend Images/Getty Images; pp. 3, 23 Faraways/Shutterstock.com; p. 4 Purestock/Thinkstock; p. 5 (book) Maximilian Laschon/Shutterstock.com; p. 7 David H. Wells/Corbis Documentary/Getty Images; p. 10 Dmitry Kalinovsky/Hemera/Thinkstock; p. 12 McCarthy's PhotoWorks/Shutterstock.com; p. 14 maggee/Shutterstock.com; p. 16 Bloomberg/Getty Images; p. 18 JNaether/Shutterstock.com; p. 20 Len Redkoles/National Hockey League/Getty Images; p. 22 ymgerman/Shutterstock.com; p. 25 Dmitry Kalinovsky/Shutterstock.com; p. 27 Joshua Rainey Photography/Shutterstock.com; p. 29 Lisa_Rivali/iStock/Thinkstock; p. 31 Frank Whitney/ Photographer's Choice/Getty Images; p. 33 Getty Images; p. 37 Christopher Halloran/Shutterstock.com; p. 39 ullstein bild/Getty Images; p. 41 Thomas Trutschel/Photothek/Getty Images; p. 45 Jenny Acheson/Iconica/Getty Images; p. 47 bluelela/Shutterstock.com; cover and interior pages icons and graphics Shutterstock.com: Anna_leni (owl), Draze Design (pad and pencil), RedlineVector (light bulb), Yuri Gayvoronskiy (eyes), james Weston (scrambled numbers), Ratoca (thumbs up), BeRad (magnifying glass).

Contents

Take your time doing word problems. Be sure to read the whole problem before trying to solve it.

Problem-Solving Tips

Word problems may seem complicated, but don't worry. Once you learn the tips and tricks in this book, they will seem simple. Let's start with these tips.

Be positive!

Start every problem knowing you can solve it. It might take more than one try, but you will learn from your mistakes.

Ask for help!

It is OK to ask for help when you don't understand something. If you ask the first time you get stuck, you will have an easier time solving future problems.

Do your homework!

The more you practice anything, the better you become at it. You can't play an instrument or play a sport well without practice. Homework problems are your practice.

In some problems, you will see clue spotters. A magnifying glass will help you spy clue words in the problem.

clue

 Move on!

If you get stuck, move to the next problem. Do the ones you know how to solve first. Go back later and try the problems you skipped.

Ask questions!

When someone is helping you, it is your chance to ask questions. If you don't ask questions, you will never get answers!

Take a break!

If you have tried everything you can think of, and you are starting to get frustrated, take a break. Take a deep breath. Stretch your arms and legs. Get a drink of water or a snack. Then come back and try again.

Don't give up!

The first time you try to solve a word problem, you might not solve it correctly. Don't give up! Check your math. Try solving the problem a different way. If you quit, you won't learn.

One Step at a Time

Word problems can be solved by following four easy steps.

? **Here's the problem.**

Three garbage trucks (each) dumped 8 tons of garbage into a pile. How much does the pile of garbage weigh?

Garbage trucks have a big job. They collect all our trash and bring it to landfills and other places. The US produces around 220 million tons of waste each year!

 Step 1 Read and understand the problem.

Read the problem carefully.
Put the problem in your own words.

What do you know?

There were 3 garbage trucks.

Each truck dumped 8 tons of garbage.

What are you trying to find?

The weight of all the garbage.

To understand the problem, ask yourself other questions, like:

What is happening in the problem? Are there any clue words? Have I ever seen a problem like this one?

Step 2 Make a plan.

Some problems tell you how they should be solved, like "draw a picture," or "write an equation." For other problems, you will need to make your own plan. Most problems can be solved in more than one way. Some plans you might try are:

Find a pattern   Write an equation

Draw a picture   Use a model

Estimate   Break it apart

How can you solve this problem?

You could draw a picture.

Step 3 Solve the problem.

It is time to do the math! If you find that your plan is not working, make a new plan. Don't give up the first time. Write your answer. Make sure you include the units.

Let's draw the picture.

Draw a simple picture to show 3 trucks with 8 tons of garbage each. You can use a large box for each truck, and small circles or squares for each ton of garbage.

Now count the number of tons of garbage that were dumped into the pile.

The pile of garbage weighs 24 tons.

Step 4 Look back.

The problem is solved! But you aren't finished yet. Take a good look at your answer. **Did you use the right numbers to begin?** Estimate or use a different operation to check your math.

Does the answer make sense?

Yes.

Did you include the units in your answer?

Yes.

Is there another way to solve the problem?

Yes, you can multiply the number of garbage trucks (3) by the weight of garbage each truck dumped (8 tons).

Try the other plan and see if you get the same answer.

3×8 tons $= 24$ tons

Either plan gives the same answer, 24 tons of garbage.

Equations

One of the things that can make a word problem easier is turning it into an equation. Equations use numbers to write a sentence.

? Here's the problem.

A skid loader made 3 trips from a truck to a warehouse. It moved 20 watermelons on each trip. How many watermelons did the skid loader move?

Skid loaders, also called skid steers, are small wheeled machines that can have different tools attached to the front. They can lift and move heavy loads.

 Read and understand.

What do you know?

The skid loader moved 20 watermelons per trip.
It made 3 trips.

What are you trying to find?

How many watermelons the skid loader moved.

Plan.

Let's find the answer by writing an equation.

Solve.

Write a sentence in words that describes the problem.

The number of trips times the number of watermelons per trip is the total number of watermelons.

Now, write the sentence using math symbols and the numbers from the problem.

3 trips × 20 watermelons per trip = total watermelons

Multiply 3 × 20 = 60

The skid loader moved 60 watermelons.

Look back.

Does the answer make sense?

Yes.

Did you start with the right numbers?

Yes.

Is This Multiplication?

Multiplication is one of the four main operations used to solve math problems. How can you tell if a word problem is a multiplication problem?

Here's the problem.

There are 5 lug nuts on each tire of a race car. During a pit stop, all 4 tires are changed. How many lug nuts are there on 4 tires?

Lug nuts are fasteners used to attach a wheel to the axles of a car or truck.

Read and understand.

What do you know?

There are 5 lug nuts on one tire. There are 4 tires on a race car.

What are you trying to find?

The number of lug nuts on 4 tires.

Are there any clue words in the problem?

Clue words are words that tell you what kind of equation you can write to solve the problem. Here are some clue words that tell you when a problem uses multiplication: **at**, **each**, **every**, **multiply**, **of**, **per**, **product**, **rate**, **times**, **twice**.

This problem uses the clue word "**each**."

In a pit crew, two people can change four tires in less than 12 seconds!

Problems that combine sets of the same size, like lug nuts per tire, are multiplication problems.

Plan.

Let's write a multiplication equation.

Solve.

Write an equation that uses the numbers from the problem, then multiply.

$$\begin{array}{r} 5 \text{ lug nuts per tire} \\ \times\, 4 \text{ tires} \\ \hline 20 \text{ lug nuts} \end{array}$$

There are 20 lug nuts on four tires.

Look back.

Is the math correct?

Yes, $5 \times 4 = 20$.

Is This Division?

Another operation used to solve problems is division. How can you tell if a word problem is a division problem, though?

Here's the problem.

An excavator dug out 48 cubic yards of dirt in 8 hours. On average, how many cubic yards of dirt did it dig in an hour?

Excavators are big digging machines. They are used for lots of jobs, such as digging trenches or foundations.

Read and understand.

What do you know?

The excavator took 8 hours to dig out 48 cubic yards of dirt.

What are you trying to find?

How many yards of dirt it dug each hour.

14

Are there any clue words in the problem?

Here are some clue words that tell you when a problem uses division: **average**, **divided**, **each**, **equally**, **evenly**, **every**, **half**, **per**, **shared**, **split**. This problem uses the clue word "**average**."

It is a division problem.

Problems that give the value (48 cubic yards) for more than one unit (8 hours) and ask for a value for one unit (one hour) are division problems.

Plan.

Let's write a division equation.

Solve.

Write an equation that uses the numbers from the problem, then divide.

48 cubic yards ÷ 8 hours = yards in one hour

$48 \div 8 = 6$

The excavator averaged 6 yards of dirt per hour.

Look back.

You can check division by using multiplication. Multiply the answer (6) by the number you divided by (8).

$6 \times 8 = 48$

If the product (48) is the number you started with, then your answer is correct. **Did you start with 48?**

Yes.

Inverse Operations

Multiplication and division are inverse, or opposite, operations.

Here's the problem.

A feller buncher cuts and stacks trees. A feller buncher operator put 36 trees into stacks of 9 trees each. How many stacks were there?

A feller buncher is a machine used in logging.
It cuts trees and gathers and stacks the logs.

Read and understand.

What do you know?

There are 36 trees. There are 9 trees in a stack.

What are you trying to find?

The number of stacks of trees.

What kind of problem is this?

The clue word "**each**" can show multiplication or division. The problem begins with a large group and divides it into stacks, so this is a division problem.

Plan.

Write a division equation.

Solve.

36 trees ÷ 9 trees per stack = number of stacks

$36 \div 9 = 4$

There were 4 stacks of trees.

Look back.

Let's look at the tree problem. From the same information, you can write two kinds of equations.

Multiplication:

4 stacks × 9 trees per stack = 36 total trees

Division:

36 total trees ÷ 9 trees per stack = 4 stacks

Because they are related, operations that are the opposites sometimes use the same clue words, like "**per**" and "**each**." The clue words will help you get started, but you must understand what is happening in the problem.

Tools That Help You Solve Problems

Draw a Picture

Drawing a picture can help you understand and solve a problem.

Here's the problem.

A snowplow took 3 minutes to clear snow from a mile of road. At this rate, how long would it take to clear 5 miles of road?

Snowplows are used to clear snow from roads, driveways, and parking lots. The big blade on the front pushes aside the snow.

Read and understand.

What do you know?

The snow plow takes 3 minutes to clear each mile of road.

What are you trying to find?

How long it will take to clear 5 miles of road.

Plan.

Let's draw a picture.

Solve.

Use a line to represent the road. Draw five sections, one for each mile. Each section takes 3 minutes to clear. Count by 3s for each section.

Count:

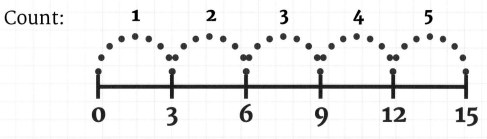

The picture helps show that 5 equal groups of 3 minutes are being combined. This is a multiplication problem.

$3 \times 5 = 15$

It would take the snowplow 15 minutes to clear 5 miles of road.

Look back.

Does the answer make sense?

Yes.

Did you start with the right numbers?

Yes.

Make a Model

You can use models, such as coins, beans, marbles, counters, or base ten blocks, to help solve a problem.

Here's the problem.

A Zamboni ice resurfacer is run 3 times during each hockey game. In one season, the fans watched the Zamboni 36 times. How many games were played that season?

The first ice resurfacing machine was designed by Frank Zamboni in 1949.

Read and understand.

What do you know?

A Zamboni runs 3 times during each game.

During the season, the Zamboni ran 36 times.

What are you trying to find?

How many games were played.

Plan.

Let's model the problem with pennies.

Solve.

Begin with 36 pennies, for the total number of times the Zamboni ran.

During each game, the Zamboni ran 3 times. Make groups of 3 pennies each to see how many games were played.

How many groups are there?

12.

There were 12 games during the season.

Look back.

Did you start with the right numbers?

Yes.

Have you seen a problem like this before?

Yes, the problem has a large group (36) that is divided into smaller ones (3).

What kind of problem is this?

It is a division problem.

Working With Ones

When a number is multiplied or divided by one, it does not change.

Here's the problem.

A street sweeper runs a route that cleans 47 streets. If it runs the route one time in a week, how many streets does it clean each week?

Street sweepers generally have big brushes attached to them. They sweep up the dirt and suck it into the truck to be thrown away.

Read and understand.

What do you know?

A street sweeper runs a route of 47 streets.
It runs the route one time in a week.

What are you trying to find?

How many streets are cleaned in a week.

Plan.

Problems that multiply any number by 1 can be solved using mental math.

Solve.

The sweeper cleans 47 streets on its route.
It runs the route one time, so multiply 47×1.

A number that is multiplied by 1 stays the same.

$47 \times 1 = 47$

The street sweeper cleans 47 streets in a week.

Look back.

Did you answer the right question?

Yes.

Does your answer make sense?

Yes.

Zeros

Zeros in a problem make multiplication and division easy!

Here's the problem.

A dump truck made 16 trips from a gravel pit to a construction site. **There were zero bananas in the truck on each trip. How many bananas did the dump truck carry in all?**

Dump trucks are made to carry loose matter in the back, such as rocks or soil. The bed tips to dump the load somewhere else.

Read and understand.

What do you know?

The dump truck made 16 trips.

On each trip, there were zero bananas in the truck.

What are you trying to find?

How many bananas the dump truck carried.

Plan.

Since the truck carried zero bananas on each trip, you can use what you know about zeros to answer the question.

Solve.

When you multiply any number and zero, the answer is always zero.

$16 \times 0 = 0$

The dump truck carried zero bananas in all.

Look back.

Does the answer make sense?

Yes.

Did you include the units in the answer?

Yes.

More Ways to Help You Solve Problems

! Find the Pattern

You can use a table to help you find patterns in information.

? Here's the problem.

In one hour, an asphalt paving truck laid 5 yards of new road. In two hours, it laid 10 yards of road, and after four hours there were 20 yards of new road. If this trend continued, how much new road was there after eight hours of work?

Compactors, or road rollers, follow the paver and smooth out the fresh tar on newly paved roads.

Read and understand.

What do you know?

The asphalt truck laid new road in these amounts:
1 hour, 5 yards; 2 hours, 10 yards; 4 hours, 20 yards.

What are you trying to find?

How much new road there was after 8 hours.

Plan.

Let's make a table.

Solve.

Make a table that organizes what you know.

Hours	1	2	4	8
Yards of New Road	5	10	20	?

The table makes it easy to see a pattern.

For each hour of work, 5 yards of new road are laid. To find the number of yards after 8 hours, multiply 5×8.

$5 \times 8 = 40$

In 8 hours, there were 40 yards of new road.

Look back.

Does the answer match the question?

Yes.

Does the answer make sense?

Yes.

Mental Tens

Problems that use powers and multiples of ten can sometimes be solved by using basic facts.

Here's the problem.

It costs about $4,000 to run a quarter-mile race in a dragster. If the race takes 4 seconds, how much does it cost per second?

Dragsters compete in races called drag races. The first car across the finish line wins.

Read and understand.

What do you know?

It costs $4,000 for a quarter-mile race.

A quarter-mile race is 4 seconds long.

What are you trying to find?

How much the race costs per second.

Some dragsters burn fuel at the same rate as fully loaded 747 jumbo jets!

Plan.

Let's write an equation.

Solve.

To find the cost per second, divide the cost you know by the number of seconds.

4,000 ÷ 4

To divide 4,000 by 4, you can use mental math and the basic fact 4 ÷ 4 = 1.

Think: Since 4 ÷ 4 = 1,   then 40 ÷ 4 = 10,
and 400 ÷ 4 = 100,
and 4,000 ÷ 4 = 1,000.

$4,000 ÷ 4 = $1,000

The race costs $1,000 per second.

Look back.

Did you start with the right numbers?

Yes.

Is the division correct?

Let's check. What is 1,000 × 4? It equals 4,000.
Yes, your division is correct.

Multiplication Equations

When there is no clue word in the problem, think about what the problem is asking.

 ## Here's the problem.

A crane was used to demolish a 15-story building. A story is 10 feet high. To smash the top of the building, how high was the wrecking ball?

Wrecking balls are often attached to cranes. Cranes can be extended to reach different heights.

Read and understand.

What do you know?
There were 15 stories in the building.
Each story is 10 feet high.

What are you trying to find?
On some problems, you can think TOO hard.
You could think, "To smash the top of the building, the ball will have to be above the building, so I'll

have to add extra to the height of the building."
This question simply wants you to find the height
of the building.

Plan.

Let's write an equation.

Solve.

One way to write a multiplication equation is to
write a sentence that uses the words "**of**" and "**is**."

_____ of _____ is _____.

15 stories of 10 feet each is the height of the
building.

Replace "**of**" with the multiplication sign and "**is**"
with the equal sign.

15 × 10 = 150

The wrecking ball was 150 feet high.

Look back.

Does the answer match the question?
Yes.

Place Value and Multiplication

Numbers with more than one digit are multiplied
one place value at a time.

A big rig has 18 wheels. There are 4 big rigs crossing a long bridge. How many wheels are on the bridge?

Big rigs, or semi-trailer trucks, often have double rows of tires to help support the heavy loads they carry.

Read and understand.

What do you know?

One big rig has 18 wheels.

There are 4 big rigs on the bridge.

What are you trying to find?

How many wheels are on the bridge.

Plan.

Let's write an equation.

Solve.

Write a sentence to describe the problem.

18 wheels on each of 4 big rigs is the total number of wheels on the bridge.

Now write it using math symbols and numbers.

$18 \times 4 =$ _____

Multiply the ones place.	Multiply the tens place.	Add.
$8 \times 4 = 32$	$10 \times 4 = 40$	$32 + 40 = 72$

18	18	18
$\times\ 4$	$\times\ 4$	$\times\ 4$
32	32	32
	40	+40
		72

$18 \times 4 = 72$

There are 72 wheels on the bridge.

Look back.

Does your answer make sense?
Yes.

How do you know? You can use estimation to check. Round 18 to 20, then multiply. $20 \times 4 = 80$, so your answer of 72 makes sense.

Division Equations

Problems that start with something large and divide it into equal parts are division problems.

 ## Here's the problem.

The space shuttle transport can travel at only 2 kilometers per hour when it is loaded. The shuttle needs to be moved 18 kilometers. How many hours will it take the transport to move the shuttle?

The space shuttle *Endeavor* took two days to travel 12 miles through the streets of Los Angeles. It was being moved to the California Science Center.

Read and understand.

What do you know?

The shuttle needs to be moved 18 kilometers.

The transport can move 2 kilometers per hour.

What are you trying to find?

How many hours it will take to move the shuttle.

Plan.

Let's write an equation.

Solve.

Each hour, the transport can move the shuttle 2 kilometers. To find how many hours the total move will take, divide the total number of kilometers (18) by how many kilometers it can move each hour (2).

18 total kilometers ÷ 2 kilometers per hour = total hours

$18 ÷ 2 = 9$

It will take 9 hours to move the shuttle.

Look back.

Did you remember to include the units in your answer?

Yes.

Place Value and Division

Numbers with more than one digit are divided one place at a time.

Here's the problem.

A box truck is used by a furniture company for deliveries. It can carry 4 couches per trip. How many trips are needed to deliver 52 couches?

Read and understand.

What do you know?

The truck can carry up to 4 couches per trip.
There are 52 couches.

What are you trying to find?

The number of trips to deliver 52 couches.

Plan.

Write a division equation.

Solve.

Divide the number of couches by the number of couches that are carried on each trip.

52 couches ÷ 4 couches each trip = number of trips

You can use the long division symbol to divide numbers with more than one digit.

52 ÷ 4 is written as $4\overline{)52}$

Divide the tens place first.
You can take 1 four from 5.

There is 1 ten left.

Bring down the ones. Divide again.

You can take 3 fours from 12.

$52 \div 4 = 13$

It will take 13 trips to deliver 52 couches.

Look back.

Did you start with the right numbers?

Yes.

Remainders

When a division problem has a remainder, you have to decide what the remainder means in the word problem.

Here's the problem.

Standing up, a monster truck tire is 66 inches tall. Standing up, a donut is about 4 inches tall. How many donuts, standing on top of each other, would it take to make a stack that is at least as tall as a monster truck tire?

This is the
monster
truck called
"Nasty Boy"
at a raceway
in Arizona.

Read and understand.

What do you know?

The monster truck tire is 66 inches tall.

A donut is 4 inches tall.

What are you trying to find?

How many donuts it takes to be at least as tall as a
monster truck tire.

Plan.

Let's draw a picture.

Solve.

Use a tall box for the tire. Draw small boxes stacked
on top of one another for the donuts.

Draw one box for every 4 inches.

16 donuts are not quite tall enough.

There is a 2-inch remainder.

$66 \div 4 = 16R2$

To be at least as tall as the tire, you need to add one more donut for those last two inches. $16 + 1 = 17$. You need 17 donuts to be at least as tall as a monster truck tire.

Look back.

Did you answer the right question?
Yes.

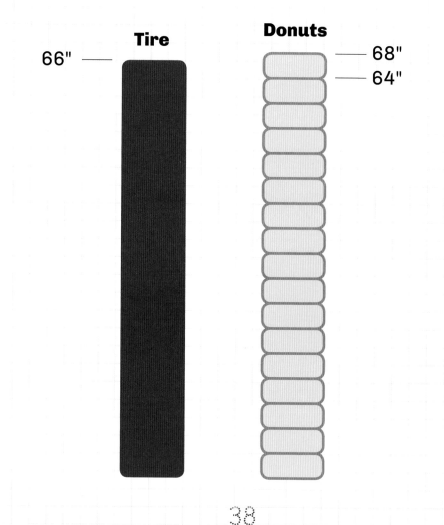

Break It Apart

Some problems use more than one operation. Try breaking the problem into simpler problems.

Here's the problem.

A road header cuts 2 feet per hour of tunnel from hard rock and 5 feet per hour from softer rock.
How long did it take to cut a tunnel that runs through 10 feet of hard rock and 20 feet of softer rock?

Road headers are used to dig tunnels or caves, or for mining. They have a cutting head that cuts or grinds away rock and other matter.

Read and understand.

What do you know?

The tunnel is dug at two speeds:

10 feet of hard rock at 2 feet per hour, and 20 feet of softer rock at 5 feet per hour.

What are you trying to find?

How long the road header took to cut the tunnel.

Are there any clue words?

Yes, more than one. The word "**per**" indicates division. The word "**and**" indicates addition.

Plan.

There are two different operations.

Let's break the problem into simpler problems.

Solve.

Divide the number of feet by the speed to find how long it took the road header to cut through the hard rock.

10 feet ÷ 2 feet per hour = 5 hours

Now find how long it took to cut through the softer rock.

20 feet ÷ 5 feet per hour = 4 hours

Now add the two partial answers together to find the total amount of time to cut the tunnel.

5 hours + 4 hours = 9 hours

It took 9 hours to cut the tunnel.

Look back.

Did you start with the right numbers?

Yes.

Estimation

Use estimation when you do not need an exact answer for a problem.

? **Here's the problem.**

A bucket-wheel excavator is used for surface mining. It is over 200 meters long. A big rig is about 18 meters long. About how many times longer is this excavator than a big rig?

Bucket wheel excavators are some of the largest vehicles on the planet. They are used as a continuous digging machine at mines.

Read and understand.

What do you know?

The length of the excavator is over 200 meters.

The length of a big rig is about 18 meters.

Bucket-wheel excavators run on 12 tracks instead of tires. Each track is as big as a school bus.

What are you trying to find?

An estimate of how many times longer the excavator is than the big rig. The problem asks "**about how many times**," so the answer does not need to be exact.

Plan.

Let's write an equation, then estimate.

Solve.

Remember, to find how many times something is larger or smaller than something else, divide the measurement of the larger item by the measurement of the smaller one.

length of excavator ÷ length of big rig

$200 \div 18 = $ _____

You can estimate the answer to a division problem by finding numbers that are close to the original numbers, but easier to divide.

Keep the 200, and change the 18 to a 20.

200 ÷ 20 = 10

A bucket-wheel excavator is about 10 times longer than a big rig.

Look back.

Did you start with the right numbers?

Yes.

Check your answer using multiplication.

10 × 20 = 200. The answer is correct.

Remember the Plan

To solve a word problem, follow these steps:

 ## Read and understand the problem.

Know what the problem says, and what you need to find.

If you don't understand, ask questions before you start.

Make a plan.

Choose the plan that makes the most sense and is easiest for you. Remember, there is usually more than one way to find the right answer.

Solve the problem.

Use the plan. If your first plan isn't working, try a different one. Take a break and come back with a fresh mind.

Look back.

Read the problem again. Make sure your answer makes sense. Check your math. If the answer does not look right, don't give up now! Use what you've learned to go back and try the problem again.

You've made it through the problems in this book. Keep practicing and you will soon be teaching your friends how to become word problem masters, too!

Glossary

addition One of the four basic operations in math; the process of adding two or more numbers together.

division One of the four basic operations in math; the process of finding out how many times a smaller number is contained within a larger one.

equation A number sentence such as $1 + 1 = 2$, where both expressions on either side of the equals sign are the same.

estimate Take a good guess.

inverse The opposite of something else. In math, addition and subtraction are inverses.

multiplication One of the four basic operations in math; the process of repeated addition.

operation A math process, such as addition, subtraction, multiplication, or division.

place value The value of a digit that is based on its position in the number.

subtraction One of the four basic operations in math; the process of taking a number away from a larger number.

unit Whatever object that is being added, subtracted, divided, or multiplied, such as cars or tons.

For More Information

Books

Adler, David A. *You Can, Toucan, Math: Word Problem-Solving Fun.* New York, NY: Holiday House, 2006.

Murphy, Stuart J. *Coyotes All Around.* New York, NY: HarperTrophy, 2003.

Scieszka, Jon. *Math Curse.* New York, NY: Viking, 2007.

Tang, Greg. *Math Potatoes: Mind-Stretching Brain Food.* New York, NY: Scholastic Press, 2005.

Websites

Aplusmath
www.aplusmath.com

Interactive math resources for teachers, parents, and students featuring free math worksheets, math games, math flashcards, and more.

Coolmath Games
www.coolmath-games.com

A fun way to practice math for students featuring free math games.

Math Playground
www.mathplayground.com/word problems.html

Features free math games, worksheets, puzzles and more.

Index